# THE STORY OF HOME

God at Work in the Bible's Tales of Home

CAROLINE SAUNDERS

B&H kids

Brentwood TN

## Dedications

### From Caroline
For Adelaide, who loves our home so much, whose
laughter and creativity make it feel like home,
who sometimes feels homesick. My sweet girl, when
you long for home, don't forget the homiest Home
and the One who built the way. I love you!

### From Jade
For my mom and dad, who welcomed me in their
home with open arms and taught me that home is a place
of love, warmth, and trust. Thank you for giving me a
glimpse of the forever Home Jesus is making for all of us.

Text copyright © 2023 by Caroline Saunders
Art copyright © 2023 by B&H Publishing Group
Published by B&H Publishing Group, Brentwood, Tennessee
All rights reserved.   978-1-0877-5669-1
Scripture quotations are taken from the Christian Standard Bible®,
Copyright © 2017 by Holman Bible Publishers. Used by permission.
Christian Standard Bible® and CSB® are federally registered
trademarks of Holman Bible Publishers.
Dewey Decimal Classification: CE
Subject Heading: HOME / BIBLE—STUDY AND TEACHING / JESUS CHRIST
Printed in Shenzhen, Guangdong, China, October 2022
1 2 3 4 5 6 · 26 25 24 23 22

There are thirty-one Scripture citations
hidden in this book. Can you find them?
Read them in your Bible to learn more
about Jesus, who is making the best Home.

In the beginning,
people lived in a
perfect home.

God had built every part of it with love:
the zebra's stripes, the wind's soft flutter,
the lemon's pucker, the fish's *blub blub*.

No one makes a home like God!

Genesis 1

God created the first man, Adam, and told him the one rule:

"There is one fruit tree I do not want you to eat from. It will destroy you."

God gave this rule because of His goodness, which was everywhere in the garden.

Genesis 2:16-25

God welcomed the first man and woman, Adam and Eve, exclaiming,

"This garden home is for you!"

But one day, the serpent wanted to ruin this home, like an intruder. He hissed, "That tree's fruit won't destroy you! It will make you like God. Why not try it?"

*Genesis 3:1-5*

Even though they knew what God had said, and even though their home proved God's love and goodness, Adam and Eve disobeyed. They ate.

*Genesis 3:6*

Suddenly, the garden didn't seem so homey anymore!
They felt icky and ashamed and pointed fingers at
each other in blame. Sin had come into the world—
and sin is the opposite of God's goodness.

Genesis 3:7–8

Adam and Eve had to leave their home, but God gave them a promise. Even though sin would keep intruding, one day, Someone would defeat sin and the serpent forever—and He would build the way to a more wonderful Home.

Genesis 3:22–24

Genesis 3:15

Years passed, and
humans could never
quite find their way Home.
They caught glimpses of it when
they spotted the zebra's stripes, felt
the wind's soft flutter, tasted the lemon's
pucker, or noticed the fish's *blub blub*.

But most of the time, sin seemed to intrude upon the whole earth. Not just around them but inside them.

Genesis 6:5

The people were so homesick! Where was the Home God had promised?

God hadn't forgotten His people! His plan was right on track, and He gave them hints of the Home that was coming.

When God's people were trapped in an unsafe home in Egypt, God made a surprising way out.

Exodus 12–14

Then God instructed them to build a tabernacle so He could be with them and remind them of the garden long ago.

Next, God guided the people to the Promised Land. It wasn't a perfect home, but it was a hint.

In the Promised Land,
God told the king,

"One day, your son
will build me a temple,
but I have an even
bigger plan than that.
It's about *My* Son
and the house *We* will
build *you*—a house that
will last forever."

What did He mean?

2 Samuel 7:12–16

So the king's son built a temple with reminders of that long-ago garden. God's glory filled the temple with a **WHOOSH!** that knocked the priests off their feet.

1 Kings 6

God's people rejoiced. No one makes a home like God!

1 Kings 8:10–11, 66

The people loved where they lived, but sin continued to settle inside their hearts. God warned them that sin destroys homes, but they did not believe Him.

Jeremiah 25:8-11

Years later, intruders came, just as God had said.
They destroyed the temple, and God's people
were taken from the Promised Land.

They were terribly homesick.

Eventually, God brought His people back, but the rebuilt temple didn't seem quite as wonderful. Wasn't there something more?

*Ezra 3:12*

God hinted,

"One day, My glory will WHOOSH! in a way you can't imagine!"

Haggai 2:3-9

Then, at just the right time, God said to His Son,

"Let's make the way Home."

19

So God's Son, Jesus, made His home on earth
as a human. Though there was sin around Him,
it never made its home inside Him.

At first, Jesus lived privately as a carpenter,
building things people could see. Later, He gave
people hints about a Home they could not see.

He spoke of a house in heaven
with many rooms.

He hugged little children and said,

"The Home I am building
is for you!"

He smiled at the poor and said,

"The Home I am building
is for you!"

John 14:2

Matthew 19:14

Luke 6:20

Jesus welcomed everyone who longed for God, for family, for love. He invited everyone who felt homesick.

Jesus warned people about the sin around them and the sin inside them.

To many people with lots of money, He said,

"You love your money more than anything, and that makes it nearly impossible for you to enter my Home."

Matthew 19:16–30

To people who were unkind to the needy, He said,

"You don't see the enemy like an intruder. Instead, you see him as a father."

John 8:44

To people gathered at the temple, Jesus said,

"Destroy this, and I will rebuild it in three days."

What did He mean?

John 2:19

Jesus's words made some people mad and other people curious.

Tired of listening to Jesus, angry people seized Him, and they grabbed wood and nails. They weren't going to build something— they were going to destroy Someone.

*John 19:15–30*

But Jesus knew this was the way. He had even told His followers,

"This is my body, given for you."

*Luke 22:19*

Then, just like the beautiful temple from long ago, Jesus's body was destroyed by intruders.

The people who loved Jesus had never, ever felt more homesick. Their hearts cried out: *What does it mean? We thought He was the way Home!* Then they laid His body in a tomb, thinking this was the end.

But they were wrong.

At the darkest moment, when it seemed the intruder had won, God told Jesus,

**"Live again!"**

And He did.

Luke 24:1–6

All along, God had been planning a way Home, and Jesus built it!

He built it by living the perfect life no other human could.

He built it with the wood of His cross and the nails in His hands, dying the death only sinners deserve.

He built it by coming back to life, shouting to the intruder,

"Get out!
You will not win!"

He built it by drawing close to the homesick, saying,

"Come Home to me!"

Seeing Jesus alive was like a big *WHOOSH!* that knocked people off their feet! It was more welcoming than the zebra's stripes, the wind's soft flutter, the lemon's pucker, and the fish's *blub blub*.

Now that He had proved God's love and goodness in every way, Jesus returned to His heavenly Home. But He told His followers,

Hebrews 1:3

"Don't worry—I will send the Holy Spirit to make His home inside you.

When the intruder asks you to sin, the Spirit will help you.

John 14:16–17, 26

When you feel alone, you will know I am with you.

When you see friends who are homesick, you can tell them the way Home.

And when *you* feel homesick,
don't forget how I love you!

Don't forget I am coming back
to set up the homiest Home."

John 14:3

This Home will be better than the garden, the tabernacle, the Promised Land, the temple, and the best earthly home we could imagine. No one makes a Home like God!

Isaiah 65:17-25

All of God's people will be together with Him, surrounded by His glory and goodness. We will feast with our family, living safely inside walls no intruder can enter, and no one will ever be homesick because we are right where we've always longed to be:

Home.

Revelation 22:1-5

## REMEMBER

"Look, God's dwelling
is with humanity, and
he will live with them. They
will be his peoples, and God
himself will be with them and
will be their God."–Revelation 21:3

## READ

The Bible's stories about home teach us important lessons, like: *No one makes a home like God. Sin destroys homes. We want to be Home with God. God wants to make His Home with His people.* These ideas piece together beautifully when we get to Jesus, the One who made the way for sinners to come Home.

*Jesus's Birth.* Read John 1:14. We could not get to God, so God came to us! Jesus "became flesh and tabernacled among us." The Old Testament tabernacle was an arrow pointing to Jesus! Both the Old Testament tabernacle and Jesus's birth give us wonderful news: God wants to make His Home with His people.

*Jesus's Life and Death.* Read John 14:23. These words can feel worrisome: We cannot obey all the way, so how can we be Home with God? Jesus made the way by living a perfect life and dying the death only sinners deserve. When we follow Jesus and trust that He died for our sins, God looks at us the way He looks at Jesus: as His loved and perfect child!

*Jesus's Resurrection and Reign.* Read John 14:3. Jesus didn't stay dead! He lives and reigns today, and He is preparing a Home for His family. No one makes a Home like God! As we wait for His return and our forever Home, His Spirit is at home in our hearts.

## THINK

1. Have you ever felt homesick? What do you miss about your home when you're away?

2. God's people suffer when they let sin make its home in their hearts. If you follow Jesus, all your sins are forgiven forever. But sin can still impact us. Is there a sin you're trying to fight? Who did Jesus send to help you fight sin?

3. Even the best earthly home isn't a perfect home. Sin is around and inside every human—and sin destroys homes, in big and little ways. When your earthly home doesn't feel homey, you can remember Jesus. What did He do to make a way for you to have a true and perfect home one day? What are you looking forward to about that home?

4. Sometimes when families welcome a new family member, they prepare a special room for that person to show their love and excitement. How does this remind you of Jesus?

5. People often feel a homesickness for God because we long to be with Him. What can you tell a homesick friend about Jesus?